MW01204531

DISCARD

ANIMAL FAMILIES

The Dog Family

CHELSEA
CLUBHOUSE

An Imprint of Chelsea House Publishers
A Haights Cross Communications ✔ Company
Philadelphia

Bev Harvey

This edition first published in 2004 in the United States of America by Chelsea Clubhouse, a division of Chelsea House Publishers and a subsidiary of Haights Cross Communications.

Chelsea Clubhouse
1974 Sproul Road, Suite 400
Broomall, PA 19008-0914

The Chelsea House world wide web address is www.chelseahouse.com

Library of Congress Cataloging-in-Publication Data

Harvey, Bev.
  The dog family / Bev Harvey.
  p. cm. — (Animal families)

  Summary: Simple text compares and contrasts members of the dog family in terms of where they live, body features, eating habits, and size. Species featured include foxes, African hunting dogs, dingoes, coyotes, black-backed jackals, gray wolves, and domestic dogs.

  ISBN 0-7910-7542-7
  1. Canidae—Juvenile literature. [1. Dog family (Mammals)] I. Title.
  QL737.C22H374 2004
  599.77—dc21

                                                                    2002155658

First published in 2003 by
MACMILLAN EDUCATION AUSTRALIA PTY LTD
627 Chapel Street, South Yarra, Australia, 3141

Associated companies and representatives throughout the world.

Edited by Angelique Campbell-Muir
Page layout by Domenic Lauricella
Photo research by Sarah Saunders

Printed in China

Acknowledgements
The author and the publisher are grateful to the following for permission to reproduce copyright material:

Cover photograph: coyote howling, courtesy of John Shaw/Auscape.

ANT Photo Library, pp. 4 (bottom), 6 (top), 6 (bottom), 11, 15, 16, 20; Ferrero-Labat/Auscape, pp. 7 (center), 24; Mike Hill—Oxford Scientific Films/Auscape, p. 10; Fritz Polking/Auscape, pp. 6 (center), 18; John Shaw/Auscape, pp. 1, 7 (top), 22; Australian Picture Library/Corbis, p. 19, 23; Coo-ee Picture Library, pp. 8–9, 29; Getty Images, pp. 4 (top), 5, 7 (bottom), 26, 27, 28; National Oceanic and Atmospheric Administration (NOAA), p. 14; Northern Territory Library, Evans Collection, p. 21; Photolibrary.com, p. 25; Ralf Schmode, p. 17.

While every care has been taken to trace and acknowledge copyright, the publisher tenders their apologies for any accidental infringement where copyright has proved untraceable. Where the attempt has been unsuccessful, the publisher welcomes information that would redress the situation.

Contents

Animal Families

Scientists group similar kinds of animals together. They call these groups families. The animals that belong to each family share similar features.

tail

pointy ears

sharp teeth

strong legs

fur

pointy ears

tail

sharp teeth

strong legs

The dog family

All kinds of dogs belong to the dog family.
Wild dogs live in forests, on plains, in swamps,
and in deserts. Pet dogs live with people.

Many people keep dogs as pets.

Where Dogs Live

Red foxes live throughout North America, Europe, and Asia. There are also red foxes in Australia and northern Africa.

Most African hunting dogs roam African plains.

Large numbers of dingoes live in Australia, and small groups are found in southeast Asia.

Coyotes live in North America.

Black-backed jackals are found along the east coast and the southern tip of Africa.

Most gray wolves are now found in only Alaska, Canada, and a few northern areas of the United States. Some gray wolves live in parts of Mexico, Europe, and Asia.

Dog Features

Members of the dog family have many features in common.

thick fur to keep warm

strong legs for running

colored fur for **camouflage**

big ears for sharp hearing

a pointed **snout** for smelling **prey**

sharp teeth for killing and eating prey

9

Dogs as Hunters

Dogs have strong legs and are good runners. Most dogs can run long distances. Some dogs hunt large prey together in **packs**. Other dogs hunt small prey on their own.

The senses of smell and hearing help dogs like foxes locate prey.

Dingoes and other dogs mainly eat meat.

Dogs are **omnivores**. They eat meat, vegetables, and fruit.

The Size of Dogs

Pet dogs can be small like chihuahuas or big like Irish wolfhounds. Foxes are the smallest and gray wolves the largest of the wild dogs.

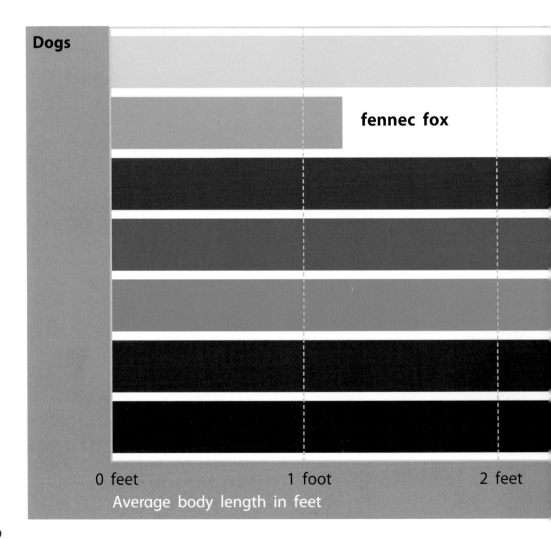

Dogs

fennec fox

0 feet   1 foot   2 feet

Average body length in feet

Dogs are measured from the tip of the nose to the end of the body.

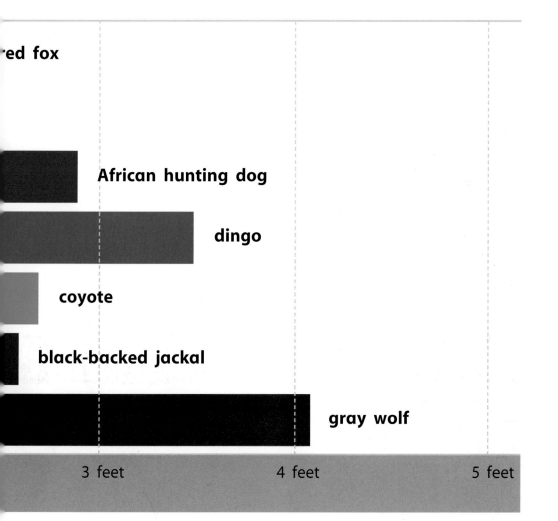

ed fox

African hunting dog

dingo

coyote

black-backed jackal

gray wolf

3 feet   4 feet   5 feet

13

Foxes

There are many kinds of foxes. Foxes have long, bushy tails. They hunt alone, mostly at night.

Foxes have pointed snouts and bushy tails.

Red foxes

The red fox has a white tipped-tail and a reddish-brown coat.

Red foxes usually hunt at night.

Fennec foxes

The fennec fox is the smallest member of the dog family. Its body is about 16 inches (40 centimeters) long. It has large, pointed ears and light tan-colored fur.

The fennec fox's large ears release body heat, so it stays cool.

Fennec foxes usually rest during the day.

The fennec fox lives in the Sahara Desert of Africa. Its **den** has lots of entrances and tunnels.

African Hunting Dogs

The African hunting dog lives in a large pack. The dogs help each other to hunt by taking turns chasing their prey.

African hunting dogs' coats have black, brown, and white patches.

African parks and reserves provide food for the dogs.

The African hunting dog is **endangered**.
There are few living in the wild any more.
Most now live in parks and **reserves** where
they are protected.

Dingoes

Most dingoes live in Australia. In the wild an adult dingo lives with its mate and pups.

Pups drink milk from their mother.

Years ago, some people kept dingoes for pets.

In the past, **Aboriginal people** took dingo pups and raised them as pets. Dingoes kept their owners warm, helped with hunting, and guarded the camp.

Coyotes

The coyote lives in desert, grassland, and mountain areas. At night it howls and **yips** to other coyotes.

A coyote's howl can be heard several miles away.

Coyotes eat mostly small animals such as mice, rabbits, or squirrels.

The coyote uses its sense of smell to track its prey. It can run fast, and for long distances, to hunt and catch its prey.

Black-backed Jackals

The black-backed jackal has a black stripe on its back that stretches from its head to its tail.

Black-backed jackals usually live in open areas rather than forests.

Pups depend on their parents for food.

When a black-backed jackal finds a mate, they stay together for many years. They have litters of about four pups at a time. The pups stop drinking milk from their mother at eight weeks.

Gray Wolves

There are two types of wolves. The gray wolf is the largest. They are usually a gray color, but they can have white, sandy, reddish, or black coats.

Gray wolves are larger than any other type of wild dog.

Most packs have five to nine members.

Gray wolves live and hunt in packs. This helps them to hunt prey much bigger than themselves. Gray wolves hunt animals such as deer, moose, and bison.

Pet Dogs

There are many **breeds** of pet dogs. Each breed has unique features. For example, poodles have tight, curly coats. Dalmatians have short, white coats with black spots.

Many people adopt puppies.

This guide dog helps
people who are blind.

Dogs help people in many ways. There
are guide dogs, police dogs, farm dogs,
and guard dogs.

Common and Scientific Names

The scientific name for the dog family is Canidae. There are 34 types of dogs in the dog family. These are the common and scientific names of the ones in this book:

Canidae family			
Common name	**Scientific names:**		
	Genus	**Species**	**Subspecies**
red fox	*Vulpes*	*vulpes*	
fennec fox	*Vulpes*	*zerda*	
African hunting dog	*Lycaon*	*pictus*	
dingo	*Canis*	*lupus*	*dingo*
coyote	*Canis*	*latrans*	
black-backed jackal	*Canis*	*mesomelas*	
gray wolf	*Canis*	*lupus*	
pet dog	*Canis*	*lupus*	*familiaris*

Glossary

Aboriginal people	a group of people native to Australia
breeds	types of animals raised by people to look a certain way or to perform certain tasks
camouflage	to blend in with surroundings so it is hard to be seen
den	a hidden place, such as a cave or a hole under the ground, where an animal lives
endangered	in danger of becoming extinct, or dying out
genus	the name for a large group of similar animals within an animal family; the genus is the first part of the scientific name of an animal
omnivore	an animal that eats both plants and meat
pack	a group of dogs that hunt and live together
prey	an animal that is hunted for food
reserves	areas of land set aside for animals to live where they are protected
snout	the long nose of an animal
species	a group of animals that are closely related and can produce young; the species is the second part of the scientific name of an animal
yips	quick sharp barks

Index